Tug of War

Tug of War

Choosing between Zion and Babylon

Mary Ellen Edmunds

DESERET
BOOK

Salt Lake City, Utah

© 2013 Mary Ellen Edmunds

DESERET BOOK is a registered trademark of Deseret Book Company.

Visit us at DeseretBook.com

Library of Congress Cataloging-in-Publication Data

(CIP on file)
ISBN 978-1-60907-056-4

Printed in the United States of America
RR Donnelley, Crawfordsville, IN

10   9   8   7   6   5   4   3   2   1

Wherefore, seek not the things of this world but seek ye first to build up the kingdom of God, and to establish his righteousness, and all these *things* shall be added unto you.

—JST, Matthew 6:38

❀

Contents

❀

CHAPTER 1

Zion: A Condition of the Heart

One of the important gifts God has given to all of His children is agency. It's something the devil wanted to take away, and it caused a war during our premortal existence. We had agency then and the freedom to choose between two plans—our Heavenly Father's Great Plan of Happiness, or the devil's plan of misery (not great at all).

It must have been quite a "tug of war," with strong discussions and persuasion among all of us as we made our choice. Ultimately, one-third of Heavenly Father's children decided to follow the devil and his plan of misery. The consequences of that choice are hard to comprehend. No body? Choosing to be a "no-body?!" Those of us who chose our Heavenly Father's Great

Plan of Happiness had the blessing of being born into this world, this earthly existence, this Second Estate, with a body. With agency. And with lots of choices.

But the war continues. We're still tugged towards Zion on the one hand (happiness, light, and peace) and Babylon on the other hand (worldliness, darkness, and misery), but the choice between the two is often not as clear-cut as these descriptions may lead us to believe. Elder Neal A. Maxwell reminded us that "the tugs and pulls of the world are powerful. Worldly lifestyles are cleverly reinforced by the rationalization, 'Everybody is doing it.'"[1]

Let's consider a fictional story, which for some may seem true because of your experiences with family or friends. You may know some who have made choices which have taken them away from the Church, from the Savior, from Zion.

A returned missionary and his sweetheart married in the temple. They had several children and were busy with their family, with their callings in the Church, and with the husband's work. After several years, they decided to "leave" the Church. Their apostasy went so far that they had their names (and their children's names) removed from Church records. They gave up their membership.

How did it happen? What led them to such a tragic decision?

Well, for one thing, they began listening to some friends who had left the Church and who said they felt "so free!" They began reading a lot of things on the Internet about people who had left the Church and who felt "so good" about their decision.

There were comments about how much nicer and relaxing Sundays were, and how much guilt had flown out the window.

But think of all the other things that had also "flown out the window." They turned away from the Savior and His Atonement. They gave up sweet communication with their Heavenly Father, the gift and guidance of the Holy Ghost, partaking of the sacrament, attending the temple, cherishing the Book of Mormon, loving the truth that families can be together forever.

Choices have consequences, and it's uncomfortable to think of what will happen to this little family if they don't change their minds and return. The scriptures tell us, "Wo unto them who are cut off from my church, for the same are overcome of the world" (D&C 50:8). They chose Babylon! They fell for the lies of worldliness "hook, line, and sinker!"

In Alma 5:57 we read, "And now I say unto you, all you that are desirous to follow the voice of the good shepherd, come ye out from the wicked, and be ye separate, and touch not their unclean things; and behold, their names shall be blotted out, that the names of the wicked shall not be numbered among the names of the righteous, that the word of God may be fulfilled which saith: The names of the wicked shall not be mingled with the names of my people."

They asked for their names to be blotted out. They are no longer numbered. They are among those whom the Savior spoke of when He said, "If he repent not he shall not be numbered among my people, that he may not destroy my people, for behold I know my sheep, and they are numbered" (3 Nephi 18:31). Maybe we should sing "When the Saints Go Marching In" differently because we *do* want to "be in that number"![2]

The Savior will keep calling to all of us, "Will ye not now return unto me, and repent of your sins, and be converted, that I may heal you?" (3 Nephi 9:13). He wants us to be numbered. The Lord calls us to come to Zion. "Behold, I, the Lord, who was crucified for the sins of the world, give unto you a commandment that you shall forsake the world" (D&C 53:2).

From the hymnbook we sing:

> Israel, Israel, God is calling,
> Calling thee from lands of woe.
> Babylon the great is falling;
> God shall all her tow'rs o'erthrow. . . .

> Come to Zion, come to Zion,
> And within her walls rejoice. . . .
> Come to Zion, come to Zion,
> For your coming Lord is nigh.[3]

Come to Zion! Come to Zion! So what *is* Zion?

It's a national park. I worked there during the summers when I was sixteen and seventeen. It was a great place to have your first experience away from home. I used to think of this beautiful park when I'd read about Zion in the scriptures. I thought it would be a swell place for the righteous to dwell.

But what is Zion *really*? Let's go back to a verse

we're all familiar with. "And the Lord called his people Zion, because they were of one heart and one mind, and dwelt in righteousness; and there was no poor among them" (Moses 7:18). And from the Doctrine and Covenants, "Therefore, verily, thus saith the Lord, let Zion rejoice, for this is Zion—the pure in heart; therefore, let Zion rejoice, while all the wicked shall mourn" (D&C 97:21).

The choice is between *rejoice* or *mourn*? I'd rather rejoice!

Zion is a place of holiness and beauty. Zion is the pure in heart in any day, any time, any place. Elder Bruce R. McConkie defined Zion this way: "Zion is people . . . those out of whose souls dross and evil have been burned as though by fire . . . so as to stand pure and clean before the Lord. Zion is those who keep the commandments of God."[4]

Gospel scholar and Brigham Young University professor Hugh Nibley observed that the two most common words used to describe Zion are *beauty* and *joy*. He referred to Zion as a place of refuge in a doomed world, but he also provided a caution. In his words: "Buildings, walls, streets, and gates—even of gold . . . do not make Zion; neither do throngs in shining robes. Zion is not a Cecil B. DeMille production. . . .

"What makes Zion? . . . Zion is the pure in heart—it is not a society or religion of . . . pious gestures and precious mannerisms: it is strictly a condition of the heart. Above all, Zion is pure, which means 'not mixed with any impurities, unalloyed'; it is all Zion and nothing else. . . . it is all pure—it is a society, a community, and an environment into which no unclean thing can enter. . . . It is not even pure people in a dirty environment, or pure people with a few impure ones among them; it is the perfectly pure in a perfectly pure environment."[5]

And what is Babylon? Simply put, it's the antithesis of Zion. Zion and Babylon are as opposite as day and night, faith and fear, good and evil, truth and lies, happiness and misery. Babylon is as dark as Zion is light! Babylon represents the world and worldliness. It represents materialism. It promotes the worshipping of false gods.

According to Elder Bruce R. McConkie, "Everything connected with [Babylon] was in opposition to all righteousness and had the effect of leading men downward to the destruction of their souls. It has become the symbol of the wickedness and evils of the world."[6]

We have so much information about the consequences of our choices. You'd think the choice between Zion and Babylon would be a "Duh!" decision. We are commanded to flee from Babylon. In fact, the Lord declares that He will not spare anyone who remains in spiritual Babylon. Yet we are still pulled towards it. There is still the fight with greed, misuse of resources, comparison, competition, selfishness, pride, the accumulation of stuff and things, waste, ego, living beyond our means, entitlements, debt, conspicuous consumption, the lure of pleasure and instant gratification, something for nothing, idolatry, etc., etc. But enough about MEE!

Why do we struggle with this? Perhaps one answer can be found in this observation from President Spencer W. Kimball: "Unfortunately we live in a world that largely rejects the values of Zion. Babylon has not and never will comprehend Zion."[7] It's a dangerous thing to try to divide our time and our hearts between

Zion and Babylon. Probably our fictional couple started out with only a "sprinkling" of Babylon in their lives—just a little bit of worldliness.

I read an article recently about a young woman who moved to a large city and became fascinated with the idea of trying out "just a little bit of worldliness." She eventually decided to see what it was like *not* to be a Mormon—just for a year. She said it was a really slow break. In her own words, "I didn't think that I would have to choose." Isn't that interesting! "I wanted to be able to make it work. I think I possibly could have. I felt that if I just met the right Mormon guy who was liberal enough, and I married him, I could stay in both worlds."

She didn't think she'd have to choose? We all have to choose! We're making choices every day. There are, after all, such tempting, intoxicating, addicting things in Babylon. It tugs at MEE! Does it ever tug at you?

For example, I have more than I need of almost everything—more clothes, more food, more books, more toys, more space, more shoes. . . . I go to a certain store (whose name I won't reveal) with coupons in hand—maybe for something I *do* need, but sometimes for things I *don't* need, because I can save three dollars and then have a ten-year supply of batteries or Scotch tape or Kleenex.

I'm making a conscious effort to turn my house from a storage unit into a home. I'm trying to cut down on the clutter. A couple of years ago I had what I called a "MEE Mall." My family came and looked through a whole bunch of useful stuff—and got great bargains (it was all free). It was pretty satisfying to watch so much stuff go out the front door. Now I'm establishing "meeBay." I'll list some things I have which I no longer need (or which I never *did* need), and the only cost to friends or family members who find something they want will be the postage!

It's easy for me to notice those who have more than I do—as if that should make me feel any better. I need to focus on all I *do* have, and be grateful, rather than whining about what I don't have. I can only consume so much—and, just as important, I can only enjoy (and use) so much. Sometimes it's difficult to follow the counsel to live within our means. I think I too often forget that I can't take it with me! I'm tugged towards that which "moth and rust" can and does corrupt.

Remember, we can never get enough of what we don't need, because what we don't need will never satisfy us. As the prophet Jacob taught: "Do not spend money for that which is of no worth, nor your labor for that which cannot satisfy. . . . Come unto the Holy One of Israel, and feast upon that which perisheth not, neither can be corrupted" (2 Nephi 9:51).

Some of you may have watched, as I did, a PBS special several years ago called *Affluenza*. It was very clever and very thought-provoking. Here's their definition of affluenza:

> *n.* an unhappy condition of overload, debt, anxiety, and waste resulting from the dogged pursuit of more.[8]

The show asked the question: How do we get people out of the malls and enjoying a life that is real? The report noted that the "work-and-spend" cycle embraced by Western civilization has *not* brought us more happiness. We're not any happier now than people were forty years ago, even though our consumption has gone up over 50 percent.[9]

No matter how hard we try to extract happiness out of material things, beyond a certain point that we call *enough*—having our needs taken care of, having some comforts and even some luxuries—more material possessions are not going to make us happy. As a matter of fact, they diminish our sense of well-being.

I ran across a phrase years ago which has stuck in my mind: *conspicuous consumption*. I've come to the conclusion that this term is used to describe accumulating goods and services mainly for the purpose of displaying income or wealth. In the mind of a conspicuous consumer, such display serves as a means of attaining or maintaining social status. It connotes consumption deliberately intended to cause envy.

Over one hundred years ago, Elder Andrew Kimball said: "I do not consider there is anything too good for the children of God, *if* we don't worship it. . . . It is the flaunting of rich clothing in such a way as to annoy those who are less fortunate in life that creates inequality and hurts the feelings of the people. I do hope, my brethren and sisters, that we will endeavor to restrain ourselves in the follies and fashions of the world."[10]

More recently, Elder D. Todd Christofferson gave us this counsel: "We might ask ourselves, living as many of us do in societies that worship possessions and pleasures, whether we are remaining aloof from covetousness and the lust to acquire more and more of this world's goods. Materialism is just one more manifestation of the idolatry and pride that characterize Babylon. Perhaps we can learn to be content with what is sufficient for our needs."[11]

I think those in Babylon seldom if ever have a feeling of contentment, tranquility, or happiness. Wouldn't we hate missing that? Babylon is bondage, even with all its present pomp and popularity.

Could you live a more contented life with fewer material possessions? Think about it. Could you? What are some obstacles that come to mind when you think about simplifying your life, reducing your spending and consumption, or giving away some of your stuff and things? It doesn't necessarily need to create a drastic change. Could you identify just one thing you'd feel comfortable doing differently to make a change in your current spending and consumption habits?

One suggestion in the *Affluenza* program was to ask ourselves some questions before we buy anything, such as:

- Do I really need it?
- Could I borrow one?
- Am I willing to dust it?

I need to clarify that I am not advocating that we should give away everything we have, be left with nothing, wear gunny sacks, and live in treehouses. But if I work hard and become rich, am I evil? Am I worldly? Am I a Babylonian? What about the promise in the Book of Mormon?

This is a very important point I want to clarify. Twenty-one times throughout the Book of Mormon a specific promise is repeated. It usually begins something like this:

"Inasmuch as ye shall keep my commandments . . ." and includes the phrase ". . . ye shall prosper in the land."

There are so many illustrations of this! As His

children kept His commandments, the Lord showered them with rich blessings, including monetary wealth. From Mosiah 2:22, we are taught that "all that he requires of you is to keep his commandments; and he has promised you that if ye would keep his commandments ye should prosper in the land; and he never doth vary from that which he hath said; therefore, if [or as] ye do keep his commandments he doth bless you and prosper you." There's also an interesting side note in verse 31: "If ye shall keep the commandments of my son, or the commandments of God which shall be delivered unto you by him, ye shall prosper in the land, and your enemies shall have no power over you."

I think it's important that along with knowing this great promise, we remember what Elder Dallin H. Oaks has taught, "The possession of wealth or the acquisition of significant income is not a mark of heavenly favor, and their absence is not evidence of heavenly disfavor."[12]

An interesting irony about our visits to Babylon is that on the one hand there may be a desire to be noticed—perhaps to be popular or famous or to live like a celebrity. Yet what often happens is that all of those in Babylon begin to be like clones. Some work very hard to look like, live like, spend like, dress like, behave like, talk like, and consume like those in Babylon.

"[One of] the major characteristics of [Babylon]," noted Stephen E. Robinson, "[is that] it seeks wealth and luxury. . . . [The] great and spacious building . . . represents the carnal world—and its values and lifestyle include mockery of the kingdom of God."[13] Let's take a look at the warning Nephi gives based on his father, Lehi's, dream: "And great was the multitude that did enter into that strange building. And . . . they did point the finger of scorn at me and those that were partaking of the fruit also; but *we heeded them not . . . for as many as heeded them, had fallen away*" (1 Nephi 8:33–34; emphasis added).

Ouch! Sadly—tragically—some who had partaken of the fruit *did* heed the mocking and the pointing . . . they acted as if they were ashamed, and they fell away into forbidden paths and were lost.

Do we heed them—the mockers? Oh, I hope not!

Have we ever joined in the scoffing, the mocking, the gossip, the pointing of fingers? (It might mean we've been "hanging out" in the Great and Spacious Building!)

Has anyone ever pointed the finger at you, accusing you of being overly religious, too obedient, too naïve? Too "goody-goody?" Some are mocked because they try to keep the Sabbath day holy, dress modestly, or avoid certain movies, music, TV shows, books, and magazines.

We are a peculiar people. But it's the gospel which makes us peculiar—unique, set apart, distinctive, uncommon. Sometimes when I teach a group of young people, I ask how many are the only Latter-day Saint student in their school, or one of the very few LDS students. Then I ask them what it's like—if it's difficult. Maybe you're the only one in your family to have joined the Church. That brings some challenges, doesn't it? Or maybe you were raised in an LDS home in an LDS neighborhood and yet have realized that there are different levels of commitment—of conversion—among your friends and family members. There may have been times when even your closest loved ones have not seemed to understand your behavior, your devotion.

There is a difference between living the gospel and merely participating in church meetings and activities, isn't there? Church meetings and activities, and even some church assignments, come to an end when we hear an "amen." But living the gospel is something for every inch and minute of our lives—for every step we take, every word we say, every thought we think. It's like an invitation put this way, "Every member a member!"

We *are* a peculiar people, which the scriptures tell us is another way of saying we're striving to be holy (see 1 Peter 2:9). One reason is for our safety and protection. We're never asked to do anything stupid—but we *are* asked to do and be that which will qualify us to return to our Heavenly Home, as opposed to that which will get us an all-expense-paid vacation in Babylon. Another reason we are asked to be holy and set apart is because we can't *do* good unless we *are* good. "A good tree cannot bring forth evil fruit, neither can a corrupt tree bring forth good fruit" (Matthew 7:18).

Years ago I was asked to speak at a fireside, and the only person I really knew was the one who had invited me. So I sat quietly and reverently at the back while I waited for her to arrive.

I was sitting behind two older women, and one turned to the other with a question. Her *S*s whistled as she asked, "Who did you say was speaking this evening?"

Her companion, also whistling her *S*s a bit, responded, "It's Mary Ellen Edmunds, and I hear she's very religious."

I almost laughed out loud. But then I began thinking about what that might mean, being "very religious." What would qualify me as a religious person? The outward things? Like attending meetings, for example. If others saw me showing up for meetings, especially every Sunday, would they think of me as being very religious?

As I pondered this experience and considered various levels of religious commitment, I was reminded of this warning from Elder Neal A. Maxwell: "While casual members are not unrighteous, they often avoid appearing to be *too* righteous by seeming less committed than they really are—an ironic form of hypocrisy. . . .

19

In contrast, those sincerely striving for greater consecration neither cast off their commitments nor the holy garment."[14]

When Lehi dreamed, he saw a great and spacious building (see 1 Nephi 8:26–27, 31–34). It was "filled with people, both old and young, both male and female; and their manner of dress was exceedingly fine; and they were in the attitude of mocking and pointing their fingers towards those who had come at and were partaking of the fruit" (v. 27).

Lehi saw other multitudes feeling their way toward the great and spacious building. He saw that once they entered they began pointing the finger of scorn at Lehi and all who were partaking of the fruit. It seems there have always been those who have become anti-light and anti-truth, and whose hearts have been stirred up to anger against that which is good (see 2 Nephi 28:20).

When I read about those in the great and spacious building pointing fingers and mocking, I remember what the Lord said to Moroni, "fools mock, but they shall mourn" (Ether 12:26). I like what Elder L. Aldin Porter wrote about this:

The wicked heap scorn when they have no other weapons to use, and too often the righteous run for cover, especially if the mocker can run fast or jump high or sing well or has high-profile degrees or a great deal of money, even if each or all have nothing to do with the subject at hand.

I ask you, what are the rewards of standing fast in your own virtue, even against the scorn of the world? They are far more monumental than one might think.[15]

That is thought-provoking for me—to consider the blessings (rewards) waiting for those who are true and faithful. At a time when the distinction between what the world values and what the gospel teaches is becoming more pronounced than ever, we need to be fully committed to living all the commandments. We cannot hold back. In a 2006 general conference address, Elder Larry W. Gibbons said: "No man can serve two masters. We cannot keep one foot in the Church and one foot in the world. We will lose our balance. . . . Let us be not 'almost' but 'altogether' Latter-day Saints."[16]

CHAPTER 2

❀

The Desires of Our Hearts

Building up the kingdom of God has been described as our preparation for the establishment of Zion. The Prophet Joseph Smith taught: "The building up of Zion is a cause that has interested the people of God in every age. . . . Show me a man or woman who has the spirit of the Gospel within them, and I will show you a man or woman whose greatest desire is to build up the kingdom of God upon the earth."[17] But at times, some of our choices may cause us to wander from those greatest desires.

> *Prone to wander, Lord, I feel it,*
> *Prone to leave the God I love;*

Here's my heart, O take and seal it;
Seal it for thy courts above.[18]

Elder Neal A. Maxwell observed that "like the prodigal son, we too can go to 'a far country.' . . . The distance . . . is not to be measured by miles, but by how far our hearts and minds are from Jesus! (see Mosiah 5:13)."[19]

Sometimes when we wander, we begin to ignore our conscience—or the discomfort in our soul—and we become less tuned in to the still, small voice. Our hearts and minds begin to move away from Jesus. In quiet times, when we're alone, we might start to feel sad. Our thoughts may lead us to consider our path and adjust our GPS. But when we have entered Babylon and are exposed to the noise and commotion of the world, some of that discomfort seems to get crowded out by competing voices.

Elder Richard G. Scott described it like this: "When things of the world crowd in, all too often the wrong things take highest priority. Then it is easy to forget the fundamental purpose of life."[20] The path to Babylon leads away from happiness, peace, safety, a clear conscience, being numbered among the Savior's sheep, and sweet relationships with family, friends, and with God. When we consider the cost of a summer cottage in Babylon, perhaps the most important factor is the location—right here . . . in our hearts.

That summer cottage might be taking up way too much space in a heart that yearns for Godliness.

We know that Zion can only be built up among those who are pure in heart. So what does it mean to be pure in heart? In part, it means to be free from that which dilutes, harms, weakens, or pollutes. To be pure is to be real and genuine. President Spencer W. Kimball said: "Zion can be built up only among those who are the pure in heart, not a people torn by covetousness or greed. . . . Not a people who are pure in appearance, rather a people who are pure in heart."[21] It's about who we are inside—not how we seem to be, or how we appear on the outside.

The people of Zion are also described as being of one heart and one mind. The scriptures tell us that they dwelt in righteousness, and there were no poor among them. (See Moses 7:18.) There are so many ways to be poor. Are we doing all we can to reach out to those in need?

Elder J. Richard Clarke tells us, "It has always been the disposition of the true disciples of Christ, as they reached higher degrees of spirituality, to look after the needy."[22] One measure of our love for the Lord is the love we show to our fellowmen by serving and blessing them in their times of need. No wonder the adversary would like us to turn our backs on those who need our help the most. "And remember in all things the poor and the needy, the sick and the afflicted, for he that doeth not these things, the same is not my disciple" (D&C 52:40). Elder Russell M. Nelson emphasized: "Few, if any, of the Lord's instructions are stated more often, or given greater emphasis, than the commandment to care for the poor and the needy. Our dispensation is no exception."[23]

Sometimes my best pondering is when I look carefully inside, not just outside. How's my heart? There are so many ways in which we can reach out to each other. Everyone in every circumstance can offer some kind of help. Before my first mission in 1962 I hadn't thought much about things like poverty. I knew I had more books, clothes, and food than some, and I also knew there were some who had lots more books, clothes, and food than I. But I didn't think much about it.

I especially didn't wonder much about whether there were any implications for me and my life because of my many blessings. Life has certainly taught me a great deal. I have met many in my life—first in Asia and eventually in Africa and other places—that I would automatically describe as poor in a material sense. As a result, much of what I thought was "the way things are" has been challenged in some deep and sometimes disturbing (and uncomfortable) ways. Now I realize that we are all poor and needy in some ways and rich in others.

To be rich has a much broader meaning than just wealth—or money—doesn't it?

Nevertheless, when we read of times when the Lord prospered His people because of their faithfulness, they did get wealthy. What did they do with their riches? How did they behave in their "exceedingly rich" situation?

In the first chapter of Alma we read, "And thus, in their prosperous circumstances, they did not send away any who were naked, or that were hungry, or that were athirst, or that were sick, or that had not been nourished" (Alma 1:30). Does this remind you of what the Savior taught in Matthew 25 about the righteous ministering to Him when He was naked, hungry, and thirsty?

"And they did not set their hearts upon riches; therefore they were liberal to all, both old and young, both bond and free, both male and female, whether out of the church or in the church, having no respect to persons as to those who stood in need. And thus [in this way] they did prosper and become far more wealthy than those who did not belong to their church" (Alma 1:30–31).

Sadly, this state of happiness lasted for only a few pages, a few chapters, a few years. Do you ever read about Zion in 4 Nephi and want to shout at the people, "Don't do it! Don't give up this great happiness that you've experienced for two hundred years! Stop it!"

I'd like to share a personal experience with the law of the fast, although I first have to say that I've not always been a "happy faster." I recall thinking of fasting as a near-death experience for most of my growing-up years, but that has all changed dramatically.

In 1974, President Spencer W. Kimball gave a general conference address in which he said, "I think that when we are affluent, as many of us are, that we . . . should be very generous and give, instead of the amount we saved by our two meals of fasting, perhaps much, much more—ten times more where we are in a position to do it."[24] Later he added that if we would give a generous fast offering, we would "increase our own prosperity both temporally and spiritually."

Aha! I'd be blessed! And I was confident it would be money! Wealth! YIPPEEEE! But it wasn't. One of the greatest blessings that has come to me as a result of increasing my fast offerings (and doing my best to be a "better faster") is that I am more aware of my blessings! This is huge!

Over the course of several years I came to a critical realization with a combination of experiences that I'll try to condense. When I'd come home from my missionary experiences in places where there was abject poverty, I'd see all my stuff and things and realize how blessed I was. I'd ask Heavenly Father: "What do you want me to do with all You have blessed me with?"

And His response to me was three things:

> Enjoy!
> Appreciate!
> Share!

Enjoy! That was the first thing. And it is so like our Heavenly Father! The second, *appreciate*, is a reminder that all that we have is really His, and He's not pleased when we don't acknowledge that fact. The third thing, *share*, includes a generous fast offering. President Marion G. Romney addressed this in a talk to seminary and institute faculty many years ago. He said: "I believe that the most practical way to protect one's self and family against economic need is to make liberal contributions for the support of the Lord's poor according to the law of the Gospel. I am not promising you riches, but I am telling you that this is the most practical way to protect yourselves and families from actual need.

"I believe that it is consistent with the laws of Heaven that one's right of reliance upon the Lord for protection against want is in direct proportion to his own liberality in sustaining the Lord's poor."[25]

It's as if we are given abundance, and then our Heavenly Father and the Savior watch us to see what we'll do with it. "I, the Lord, stretched out the heavens, and built the earth, my very handiwork; and all things therein are mine. And it is my purpose to provide for my saints, for all things are mine. . . . For the earth is full, and there is enough [we've heard that word before, haven't we?] and to spare; yea, I prepared all things, and have given unto the children of men to be agents unto themselves. Therefore, if any man shall take of the abundance which I have made, and impart not his portion, according to the law of my gospel, unto the poor and the needy, he shall, with the wicked, lift up his eyes in hell, being in torment" (D&C 104:14–15, 17–18).

He has made us agents! He has given us abundance! And we are accountable to Him for what we do with our abundance. President Spencer W. Kimball stated: "Zion is to be in the world and not of the world, not dulled by a sense of carnal security, nor paralyzed by materialism."[26] Elder D. Todd Christofferson explains further: "Throughout history, the Lord has measured societies and individuals by how well they cared for the poor. . . . We control the disposition of our means and resources, but we account to God for . . . stewardship over earthly things."[27]

It's often hard for us as "earthlings" to imagine wealth as anything besides money (and stuff and things), but "when you look at others with their lands and gold"—their shiny new cars, their extraordinarily landscaped yards, their summer cottage in Babylon—"Think [remember] that Christ has promised you his wealth untold."[28]

CHAPTER 3

❀

What Do We Teach
Our Families?

What do we teach our children when we hold on to the "summer cottage in Babylon" in spite of all we say about the importance of Zion? We've been warned that "we live in a season when fierce men do terrible and despicable things. . . . We live in a season of arrogance. We live in a season of wickedness, pornography, immorality.

"All of the sins of Sodom and Gomorrah haunt our society. Our young people have never faced a greater challenge. We have never seen more clearly the lecherous face of evil."[29]

How sad it would be if our attitude toward abundance contributed to the challenges that our children face in today's world.

Consider what a parent who chooses to spend two thousand dollars per season on clothing for a toddler is teaching his or her child. Or, as I recently heard in the news, seventeen thousand dollars on a birthday party for a ten-year-old. Are we teaching our children that what they own and what they wear and how much stuff they have is more important than who they are? Have we made the mistake of starting our children on the road to making sure they have more and better than others?

Studies show that children who have been given too much—who have been overindulged—tend to grow up to be adults who have difficulty coping with life's disappointments. They feel entitled. In other words, they become vulnerable to the crippling lie that is at the core of the adversary's plan of misery—that there is something for nothing.

Are we convincing our children that they can and should have anything they want right now? Are they missing the critical lesson of saving, of waiting, of delaying gratification and of realizing that there are some things they just cannot have or cannot do?

Elder Robert D. Hales told of an experience when

he wanted to buy his wife a beautiful dress that was not in the family budget. She simply said, "We can't afford it." Then he said: "Those words went straight to my heart. I have learned that the three most loving words are 'I love you,' and the four most caring words for those we love are 'We can't afford it.'"[30]

That phrase, "We can't afford it," can refer to much more than just "we don't have the money." Unfortunately some children are never taught that there are some things they just cannot afford.

What do children learn if they never have to work for anything—not for clothing, shoes, makeup, piano lessons, not for a cell phone, or the use of a car? The ability to wait as opposed to giving in to instant gratification may be more important in our choices, in our use of agency, than we realize.

Consider how your parents helped you learn the value and importance of working for something you wanted. You may remember some specific things they did to help you understand that you couldn't ever get something for nothing. If you're like me, you may also remember that you weren't exactly thrilled about this part of life at first, especially if you had friends and classmates who didn't have to work the way you did.

When I was about fourteen years old, I saw something in the window at Woods's store on Main Street that I really, really wanted: a pair of genuine Red Wing hiking boots. I skipped all the way home to tell Mom and Dad about them. They would be perfect for "field day" at school! They were only $14.25 (or something like that).

My parents' response wasn't quite what I had expected. "They sound wonderful. What can we do to help you earn the money?"

What? How hard can it be for parents to give their precious little daughter enough money for some hiking boots?

But I realized they were serious, so I got to work. I was already doing quite a bit of babysitting, and I continued with that. I also began selling night crawlers. I made my own sign to nail on a tree in our front yard: "Fish Bait, 15 cents a dozen."

I had boxes and dirt and wet gunny sacks to keep my worms happy and healthy. One day I got an idea and pulled some apart, and both halves lived! I doubled my profits with that one amazing discovery! I tried thirds, but that didn't work—the middle never survived. Slowly but surely I reached my goal: $14.25. I went to Woods's store and tried the boots on. It felt great to pull those leather laces together. I walked around, looking in the mirror and pretending I was already at field day, imagining how excited everyone was to see my brand-new Red Wing hiking boots. Eventually I went to the counter, and I exchanged not just my $14.25, but part of myself. There was something different about having worked so hard for something. I know you have had similar experiences and can relate to what I was feeling.

They wrapped the boots in tissue paper and put them in the official Red Wing box. Oh, my! I walked carefully all the few blocks home being careful not to get hit by a car or anything.

I wanted to wear the boots to church, but Mom put her foot down on that idea (kind of a pun there, huh?). I'd put them on for a while, then take them off, wipe them carefully, wrap them in the tissue paper, and put them back in the box.

And of course I did wear them for field day, and I

wore them during the two summers I worked at Zion National Park and on every other possible occasion. As the years went by, some of my younger brothers and sisters used them, and even some nieces and nephews.

In 1981, I returned from a long trip in southeast Asia, and my mother told me she had a surprise for me. The hiking boots! She'd had them resoled, had put new laces in, and shined them. That touched me so much!

I still have the boots. You see, they became a symbol between me and my parents of working for what I received. I think if my parents had just purchased the boots for me—which they probably could have done—I would not even remember them now.

As you remember some of your own experiences, share them with your children and others. Let them know how much you value the blessings that come from working. Be an example of this important aspect of the gospel.

Elder L. Tom Perry has given us wise counsel about the value of delayed gratification. He said: "There is a strong correlation between the success of nations and their knowledge and obedience to God's commandments. His commandments stress education (see D&C 88:118); freedom and agency (see D&C 58:28); delayed gratification and an emphasis on matters of eternal, not worldly, value (see Matthew 6:19–21; Luke 16:20–31); trust in the Lord (see 2 Nephi 4:34); and hard work (Moroni 9:6). . . .

"*Consider how much time you spend in pursuit of material possessions.* Our uncontrolled appetites and consuming drive for material gain are sending our nation on a downward spiral, and many members of the Church are going along for the ride. What has happened to the values of thrift, industry, economy, and frugality? When was delayed gratification displaced by instant gratification? . . .

"I wonder what kind of signals we are sending to our children when we purchase homes that are status symbols. . . . Such examples from parents only feed the philosophy of 'I want it now' in their children. Lost to the next generation is the discipline associated with delayed gratification."[31]

So what do we teach our children? We teach them truth. We help them learn to make wise choices. We help them feel and recognize the Spirit. Trust your common sense. Be an example! Live a simple, compassionate life. Be kind, be patient, take care of other people. Be grateful and content.

The way we spend our time and our money is an indication of the kind of life and world we want. The blessing of working together to make our homes a place of goodness, a place of holiness, a place of peace, a place of refuge and protection—is Zion!

CHAPTER 4

❁

"In the World,
But Not of the World"

Throughout the scriptures, the Lord has been abundantly clear that "[His] kingdom is not of this world" (John 18:36). "Love not the world, neither the things that are in the world. If any man love the world, the love of the Father is not in him. For all that is in the world, the lust of the flesh, and the lust of the eyes, and the pride of life, is not of the Father, but is of the world" (1 John 2:15–16).

Yet the world is where we were sent to spend our mortality. This is our home for now. This is where we'll gain experience and make critical choices. So what is the difference between being *in* the world, but not *of* the world? How do we make that distinction?

Perhaps it would help us to think of Zion as Hugh

Nibley described it, "the bridge between the world as it is, and the world as God designed it and meant it to be."[32] We can separate ourselves from worldly influences, but not from the world we live in. We can't let our "light so shine" if we isolate ourselves from our fellow travelers and put our light under a bushel. In the world, we can make positive contributions to our family, to our neighbors, and the community, but we do that in large measure by the way we live and the way we treat others. We really *can* make the world a better place.

So how do we evaluate how we're doing in this "tug of war"? How do we know if we need to make some changes? This topic requires some honest, deep soul searching regarding our allegiance to the kingdom of God. Are we too easily distracted by the world or pulled away from spiritual nourishment by the enticements of the world?

Elder Richard G. Scott identified a power tool that the devil uses against us. "He [the devil] would have good people fill life with 'good things' so there is no room for the essential ones."[33]

Perhaps we have unconsciously been caught in

that trap. I know there are times when I have struggled with priorities. At times we've all had things about which we've said, "Oh, that's no big deal." But does this ever include things which *are* a big deal? Has Zion sometimes become a tiny three-hour island on Sunday, surrounded by the rest of the week in Babylon?

Elder Neal A. Maxwell cautioned, "Many individuals preoccupied by the cares of the world are not necessarily in transgression. But they certainly are in diversion and thus waste 'the days of [their] probation' (2 Ne. 9:27). . . . while some proudly live 'without God in the world' (Alma 41:11)."[34]

Perhaps this list of questions will help in your self-evaluation process:

- Do I live without God too much of the time?
- Am I making too many compromises or doing too much rationalizing?
- Do I feel and express sincere gratitude?
- What am I struggling to let go of in the world— in Babylon?

Sooner or later (hopefully not *too* late), we will discover that every single thing the Lord has asked of us has been designed to bless us, to protect us, to make us good, to make us happy, to make us holy. "We have the promise, if we seek first the kingdom of God and [His] righteousness, that all necessary things will be added to us. We should . . . learn how to . . . build up the kingdom, and establish the Zion of our God. Then there is not the least danger, and there should not be the least doubt but what *everything necessary* for the comfort, convenience, happiness, and salvation of the people will be added to them."[35]

Are there some ways in which we can draw closer to Zion? Let's examine our hearts, our habits, our choices. What is it we love most? What would we give up in order to come closer to God, to know Him?

As I considered these questions, one strong impression that came to me was to keep the Sabbath day holy. I'm convinced this can provide for us an oasis—a rest, a break—from all that we're bombarded with through the week. We might decide to go to the temple more often than we were able to go last year, and think of specific ways in which we can be better prepared to enjoy the experience and be responsive to spiritual impressions. If there were ever a place where the difference between Babylon and Zion is most apparent, it is in this holy place—this refuge, this house of God.

We understand that "to come to Zion, it is not enough for you or me to be *somewhat* less wicked than others. We are to become not only good, but *holy* men and women."[36] We need to take time to be holy—to free ourselves from the world and the strong and alluring influences which are all around us and do as the Lord counseled Emma Smith, "lay aside the things of this world, and seek for the things of a better" (D&C 25:10).

Think of the implications—the consequences—of our exercise of agency as we are daily tugged between Zion and Babylon. "We do not need to adopt the standards . . . and the morals of Babylon. We can create Zion in the midst of Babylon. We can have our own standards for music and literature and dance and film and language . . . for dress and deportment, for politeness and respect. We can live in accordance with the Lord's moral laws. We can limit how much of Babylon we allow into our homes by the media of communication.

"We *can* live as a Zion people, if we wish to. Will it be hard? Of course it will, for the waves of Babylonian culture crash incessantly against our shores. Will it take courage? Of course it will. . . .

"And with the encroachment of Babylon, we have to create Zion in the midst of it. . . . If we are to have Zion in the midst of Babylon, we will need courage."[37]

If this promised Zion seems to be a little beyond our reach, please take encouragement from these prophetic words: "We need to understand that as much virtue can be gained in progressing toward Zion as in dwelling there. It is a process as well as a destination. We approach or withdraw from Zion through the manner in which we conduct our daily dealings, how we live within our families, whether we pay an honest tithe and generous fast offering, how we seize opportunities to serve and do so diligently. Many are perfected upon the road to Zion who will never see the city in mortality."[38]

Our souls, our spirits, seek the safety, peace, and blessings of Zion, and God will help us if this is truly the desire of our hearts. We *can* live as a Zion person and family if we really want to. Ultimately, we will

45

end up where we'll feel most comfortable—and it will either be Zion . . . or somewhere else.

The Lord said to Noah: "And the [rain]bow shall be in the cloud; and I will look upon it, that I may remember the everlasting covenant, which I made unto thy father Enoch; that, when men should keep all my commandments, Zion should again come on the earth, the city of Enoch which I have caught up unto myself. And this is mine everlasting covenant, that when thy posterity *shall embrace the truth, and look upward,* then shall Zion look downward, and all the heavens shall shake with gladness, and the earth shall tremble with joy" (JST, Genesis 9:21–22; emphasis added).

As we seek the things of a better world, let's embrace the truth and look upward!

Let our choice be clear:

> *Come to Zion, come to Zion,*
> *And within her walls rejoice. . . .*
> *Come to Zion, come to Zion,*
> *For your coming Lord is nigh.*[39]

Notes

1. Neal A. Maxwell, "The Tugs and Pulls of the World," *Ensign,* November 2000, 35–37.
2. Traditional, "When the Saints Go Marching In," available at http://www.heritagecountrychoir.com/PDF/PdfSheetMusic/WhenTheSaintsGoMarchingIn.pdf; accessed 14 November 2012.
3. Richard Smyth, "Israel, Israel, God Is Calling," *Hymns of The Church of Jesus Christ of Latter-day Saints* (Salt Lake City: The Church of Jesus Christ of Latter-day Saints, 1985), no. 7.
4. Bruce R. McConkie, *Millennial Messiah: The Second Coming of the Son of Man* (Salt Lake City: Deseret Book, 1982), 286.
5. Hugh Nibley, *Approaching Zion: The Collected Works of Hugh Nibley,* vol. 9 (Salt Lake City and Provo: Deseret Book and FARMS, 1989), 26.
6. Bruce R. McConkie, *Mormon Doctrine,* 2nd ed. (Salt Lake City: Bookcraft, 1966), 68–69.
7. Spencer W. Kimball, "Becoming the Pure in Heart," *Ensign,* May 1978, 79.

8. John De Graaf, David Wann, and Thomas H. Naylor, *Affluenza,* 2nd ed. (Berrett-Koehler Publishers, 2005), Kindle edition, introduction.

9. Ibid.

10. Andrew Kimball, in Conference Report, October 1911, 82; emphasis added.

11. D. Todd Christofferson, "Come to Zion," *Ensign,* November 2008, 37–40.

12. Dallin H. Oaks, *Pure in Heart* (Salt Lake City: Deseret Book, 1988), 75.

13. Stephen E. Robinson, "Warring against the Saints of God," *Ensign,* January 1988, 35, 37.

14. Neal A. Maxwell, "'Settle This in Your Hearts,'" *Ensign,* November 1992, 65.

15. L. Aldin Porter, "But We Heeded Them Not," *Ensign,* August 1998, 7.

16. Larry W. Gibbons, "Wherefore, Settle This in Your Hearts," *Ensign,* November 2006, 102, 103.

17. Joseph Smith, *Joseph Smith,* in Teachings of Presidents of the Church series (Salt Lake City: The Church of Jesus Christ of Latter-day Saints, 2007), 186.

18. Robert Robinson, "Come, Thou Fount of Every Blessing," *Hymns: The Church of Jesus Christ of Latter-day Saints* (Salt Lake City: The Church of Jesus Christ of Latter-day Saints, 1948), no. 70.

19. Neal A. Maxwell, "The Tugs and Pulls of the World," *Ensign,* November 2000, 35–37.

20. Richard G. Scott, "First Things First," *Ensign,* May 2001, 7.

21. Spencer W. Kimball, "Becoming the Pure in Heart," *Ensign,* May 1978, 79.

22. J. Richard Clarke, "The Storehouse Resource System," *Ensign,* May 1978, 82.

23. Russell M. Nelson, "In the Lord's Own Way," *Ensign,* May 1986, 26.

24. Spencer W. Kimball, in Conference Report, April 1974, 184.

25. Marion G. Romney, "A Practical Religion," address to seminary and institute faculty, Brigham Young University, 13 June 1956, 15; cited in Neil K. Newell, "Fast Offerings: Blessings We Give, Blessings We Receive," *Ensign,* October 1998, 21.

26. Spencer W. Kimball, "Becoming the Pure in Heart," *Ensign,* May 1978, 79.

27. D. Todd Christofferson, "Come to Zion," *Ensign,* November 2008, 37–40.

28. Johnson Oatman, Jr., "Count Your Many Blessings," *Hymns of The Church of Jesus Christ of Latter-day Saints* (Salt Lake City: The Church of Jesus Christ of Latter-day Saints, 1985), no. 241.

29. Gordon B. Hinckley, "Living in the Fulness of Times," *Ensign,* November 2001, 4–6.

30. Robert D. Hales, "Becoming Provident Providers Temporally and Spiritually," *Ensign,* May 2009, 8.

31. L. Tom Perry, *Living with Enthusiasm* (Salt Lake City: Deseret Book, 1996), 39, 42–43, 91.

32. Hugh Nibley, *Approaching Zion: The Collected Works of Hugh Nibley,* vol. 9 (Salt Lake City and Provo: Deseret Book and FARMS, 1989), 1.

33. Richard G. Scott, "First Things First," *Ensign,* May 2001, 7.

34. Neal A. Maxwell, "The Tugs and Pulls of the World," *Ensign,* November 2000, 35–37.

35. Brigham Young, in *Journal of Discourses,* 26 vols. (Liverpool:

Latter-day Saints' Book Depot, 1854–86), 7:132; emphasis added.

36. D. Todd Christofferson, "Come to Zion," *Ensign*, November 2008, 39; emphasis added.

37. David R. Stone, "Zion in the Midst of Babylon," *Ensign*, May 2006, 91–92; emphasis added.

38. Robert D. Hales, "Welfare Principles to Guide Our Lives: An Eternal Plan for the Welfare of Men's Souls," *Ensign*, May 1986, 30.

39. Richard Smyth, "Israel, Israel, God Is Calling," *Hymns*, no. 7.